The Scarlet Thread of Redemption

From Garden to Glory: The Redemption Story of the Bible

By Matthew Allen, Russ Robins and Kyle Fletcher

© 2025 Spiritbuilding Publishers.
All rights reserved. No part of this book may be reproduced in any form without the written permission of the publisher.

Published by
Spiritbuilding Publishers
9700 Ferry Road, Waynesville, Ohio 45068

THE SCARLET THREAD OF REDEMPTION
From Garden to Glory: The Redemption Story of the Bible
By Matthew Allen, Russ Robins and Kyle Fletcher

Scripture quotations taken from the Holy Bible, New International Version NIV. Copyright 1973, 1978, 1984, 2011 by Biblica, Inc.™ Used by permission. All rights reserved worldwide.

ISBN: 978-1-964-80541-2

Spiritbuilding
PUBLISHERS

spiritbuilding.com

Table of Contents

Foreword 1
Preface 3
Introduction 4
How to Use This Book 6

Part One **Foundations of Redemption** 9
Chapter 1   Perfection to Perfection 10
Chapter 2   The Rise of Satan 12
Chapter 3   The First Blood 14
Chapter 4   The Faithful Remnant Begins 16

Part Two   **The Covenant Path** 19
Chapter 5   Judgment and Grace 20
Chapter 6   Chosen By Grace 22
Chapter 7   Substitution: Isaac on the Altar 24
Chapter 8   Providence in Egypt 26

Part Three   **The Blood That Frees** 29
Chapter 9   The Blood of the Lamb 30
Chapter 10   The Tabernacle and Sacrifice 32
Chapter 11   The Wilderness Test 34
Chapter 12   Rahab and the Scarlet Cord 36
Chapter 13   Kings, Sin, and Prophets 38
Chapter 14   Foreshadowing the Cross 40

Part Four   **The Coming of the Redeemer** 43
Chapter 15   The Lamb Has Come 44
Chapter 16   The Lamb Takes Our Place 46
Chapter 17   Risen and Reigning 48
Chapter 18   The Gospel Goes Out 50
Chapter 19   Atonement Explained 52
Chapter 20   The Final Victory 54
                      Your Place in the Story 56
Author Biographies 57

Foreword

This week has been difficult. Today, as I begin this book, my heart feels heavy. On this day, we are laying my mother to rest. The funeral service begins in about two hours. I know friends and family will be there, and it will be beautiful, but I will miss her.

Her passing has inspired me to put my thoughts into words as I reflect on her life and my own. Over the past week, we've been busy gathering pictures of my mother and father, and memories have come flooding back of a beautiful couple rooted in their faith in God and His promises. I often think about my father, his loving heart, and the leadership he provided to our family and the church. My mom, his supporter and tireless worker, who raised her family and served God.

Today, we celebrate their lives with joy. It is a celebration rooted in the comfort and peace that come from knowing their walk of faith has now ended. Their faith has become sight, and they have received the reward promised by a Father who has loved them every step of the way. They are at home. Everything was made possible because of a loving God who planned a course of redemption before the foundation of the world. That plan was for my parents, for you, for me, and for everyone who has ever walked on the face of this earth.

Sadly, evil has caused many to see God not as a loving father but as a righteous judge and lawgiver, demanding our obedience. Many perceive God as one who takes away our liberties and freedom. We live in fear of eternal loss. We're afraid of failing to meet His standards, as if He looks forward to punishing those who choose a life of darkness. Sadly, many simply walk blindly into the darkness.

The hope of eternal life with God is found in the pages of the Bible you hold in your hands. Many find it hard to read through their Bibles and uncover the truths within. The early stories of Genesis and Exodus reveal a lot about early human history. However, moving through the books of law, poetry, and prophecy can sometimes cause readers to lose their way within the biblical text. As a result, the main themes and overall message can become unclear. I hope to highlight key parts of scripture and help paint a beautiful picture of a gracious God.

This book, while not exhaustive, can help us understand God's story: a Father who loves His children, a protector who has watched over us throughout our lives because He is eager for us to come home, a guide who has been with us every moment of every day, and a provider who has prepared a home for us beyond our wildest dreams.

Join us in this study of God and His work from the beginning of time to love His children and show us the way home. Thanks to my father and mother for helping me see the beautiful picture of God and the plans He has for all of us who love Him. All because God loved us before the foundation of the world. (Eph. 1:4)

> *What a day it will be, when we enter that special place, he has prepared for us. I live to hear those beautiful words someday: "Welcome home!"*

—Russ Robins

Preface

There is a thread that runs through the Bible, sometimes visible, sometimes hidden, but always present.

It begins in a garden with a single act of disobedience and traces its way through altars and blood, covenants and kings, prophets and promises. It weaves through slavery and rescue, wilderness and worship, exile and hope. It wraps around a cross on a hill and flows into an empty tomb. And it doesn't stop there.

This thread is not made of words or ideas. It is stained with blood, the blood of a Lamb who was slain.

This book is about that thread. Not a commentary on every book of the Bible, but a focused journey through the storyline of redemption. Each chapter follows a pivotal moment where the grace of God breaks through, making the coming of Christ clearer.

You won't find a list of doctrines or a textbook on theology. What you will find is a story, God's story. And, by grace, it can become yours too.

—*Matthew Allen*
June 2025

Introduction

The Bible might seem like a collection of unrelated stories without a clear message or purpose. It's understandable why some people see "The Book" this way. The Bible includes 66 separate writings, 39 in the Old Testament and 27 in the New Testament, created over 1,500 years in three different languages: Aramaic, Hebrew, and Greek. Its inspired texts were written by 40 authors from varied backgrounds, such as shepherds, farmers, tent makers, doctors, fishermen, prophets, priests, and kings.

However, the truth is, the Bible presents a single **unified story: God's plan to redeem the world through Jesus Christ.**

From start to finish, Genesis to Revelation, the Bible's story is about Jesus. The books of the law, prophecy, poetry, the gospels, and the apocalyptic language all focus on the Lamb of God. After His resurrection, Jesus explains this to His disciples: *"He said to them, 'This is what I told you while I was still with you: Everything must be fulfilled that is written about me in the Law of Moses, the Prophets, and the Psalms.'"* (Luke 24:44)

The common thread running through the Bible story is **blood.**

From the animals that covered Adam and Eve's shame to the sacrifices at the tabernacle.

From the lamb at Passover to the suffering servant in Isaiah.

From the blood-stained cross to the blood-washed saints in Revelation.

This thread ties it all together.

In this book, you'll go through twenty lessons, each revealing how God has been working His plan of salvation through Jesus Christ from the very beginning. You'll see how every part of Scripture points toward the Lamb of God, whose blood takes away the sin of the world.

Each chapter features a clear lesson, key scriptures, a reflection question, and a journal prompt to help you respond personally. Whether you're studying alone, teaching a class, or reading with a friend, it's designed to deepen your faith and improve your understanding of the gospel.

This isn't just a study of what God has already done; it's an invitation to trust in what He continues to do—and to follow the scarlet thread all the way to the Lamb who rules forever.

—Kyle Fletcher
June 2025

How to Use This Book

This book is designed to help you trace the story of redemption from Genesis to Revelation through 20 key moments tied together by the blood of Christ.

Each chapter includes:

- A clear summary of a pivotal event or passage
- Key Scriptures to reflect on and explore
- A core lesson that reveals God's redemptive purpose
- A **Reflection Question** to help you think more deeply
- A **Journal Prompt** to guide personal application

For Personal Study:

Read one chapter at a time. Sit with the Scripture references. Use the journal prompts to pray, write, and reflect. Let each lesson draw you closer to the Lamb of God.

For Small Groups or Classes:

Use each chapter as a weekly guide. Read together, discuss the reflection questions, and invite participants to share from their journaling if they're comfortable. Keep the focus on Christ and how His blood shapes our story.

For Teaching or Preaching:

Each chapter can be adapted into a lesson, sermon, or devotional message. The structure is flexible and rooted in Scripture. Feel free to expand with your own study.

This book serves as an invitation. Let the scarlet thread guide you to the cross, the empty tomb, and the throne of the Lamb.

Part One

Foundations of Redemption

Chapter 1
Perfection to Perfection
Genesis 1–2

God saw all that He had made, and behold, it was very good, Genesis 1:31

In the beginning, there was only God.

Then, with a word, He created everything. Not from raw materials, not from chaos, but from His own will and power. *"In the beginning, God created the heavens and the earth"* (Genesis 1:1).

The earth began as a dark, formless void. But God brought order. On Day One, He created light. Then, day by day, He formed a world of beauty, balance, and purpose.

- Day 1: Light and darkness
- Day 2: Sky and sea
- Day 3: Land, plants, and trees
- Day 4: Sun, moon, and stars
- Day 5: Fish and birds
- Day 6: Animals, and then, humanity

On Day Six, God created mankind, both male and female, in His own image. That's the pinnacle of creation. He didn't just create people; He gave them identity, worth, and purpose. He blessed them, entrusted them with stewardship over the earth, and declared that everything was *very good* (Genesis 1:31).

Genesis 2 focuses on the creation of man and woman. God formed Adam from the dust of the ground and breathed life into him. Later, He made Eve from Adam's side. God Himself officiated the first marriage, establishing it: *"A man shall leave his father and his mother and hold fast to his wife, and they shall become one flesh"* (Genesis 2:24).

They lived in a garden called Eden, a perfect place with no shame, pain, or death. God walked with them. Work was fulfilling. Relationships were complete. This was the world as it was intended.

But it wouldn't last. A test was coming. A voice would whisper. A lie would be believed. And the world would change.

Yet even as the fall approaches, the big picture of the Bible reminds us of something powerful: the story begins in perfection and ends in it, too.

The final chapters of Scripture depict a restored creation, a new Eden, a place without curse, tears, or death. *"Behold, the dwelling place of God is with man"* (Revelation 21:3).

God hasn't changed His purpose. He's still preparing a home for His people. The question is: will we follow the path He's made back to it?

Key Scriptures:
- *Genesis 1:26–27*, "Let Us make man in Our image"
- *Genesis 2:7*, "and breathed into his nostrils the breath of life."
- *Revelation 21:1–4*, "a new heaven and a new earth … no more death or mourning or crying or pain."

Lesson: God's design was perfect from the start. He created us for relationship, purpose, and joy in His presence. The rest of the Bible shows how He restores what was lost.

Reflection Question: What does it mean to you that you were created in the image of God?

Journal Prompt: Describe the kind of world you think Eden must have been. What do you most long to see restored in your own life or the world around you?

Chapter 2
The Rise of Satan
Genesis 3–4; Revelation 12; 1 John 2:16

> *The great dragon was hurled down, that ancient serpent called the devil, or Satan, who leads the whole world astray. He was hurled to the earth, and his angels with him,* Revelation 12:9

Genesis 3 begins with an unexpected disruption in paradise. A serpent appears, sly and calculating, speaking to Eve. Its question is subtle but dangerous: 'Did God actually say, 'You shall not eat of any tree in the garden'?" (Genesis 3:1)

But this serpent isn't just an animal. Revelation 12 reveals who he really is, Satan. Once a glorious angel named Lucifer, he rebelled against God and was cast out of heaven. He became the adversary of God and the enemy of mankind.

Thrown to the earth, Satan unleashes his fury on the first humans. If he cannot defeat God directly, he will try the next best thing: destroy God's children.

He entices Eve with a half-truth and then a blatant lie. He appeals to her desire for knowledge and power. *"You will not surely die ... you will be like God."* Eve eats, and then Adam follows.

Sin enters the world. Immediately, shame takes hold. They cover themselves. They hide from God. Fear replaces peace.

When God finds them, He pronounces judgment, but He also offers a promise. Speaking to the serpent, God says: *"I will put enmity between you and the woman, and between your offspring and her offspring; he shall bruise your head, and you shall bruise his heel"* (Genesis 3:15).

This is the first prophecy of the gospel. One day, a descendant of Eve would crush the serpent's head. Satan would wound Him but not defeat Him. That offspring is Jesus.

The consequences of sin are devastating. Adam and Eve are expelled from the garden. Their access to the tree of life is cut off. Death begins its slow march.

In Genesis 4, sin spreads. Their son Cain becomes the first murderer, killing his brother Abel out of jealousy. But even in that dark moment, a new hope arises, and Seth is born. And "people began to call on the name of the Lord" (Genesis 4:26).

The fight between good and evil has started. But so has the scarlet thread of redemption, the promise that God will succeed.

Key Scriptures:
- *Genesis 3:6–7*, "She took of its fruit and ate ... then the eyes of both were opened."
- *Genesis 3:15*, "He shall bruise your head, and you shall bruise his heel."
- *Revelation 12:9*, "The deceiver of the whole world ... was thrown down to the earth."

Lesson: Satan's lies led to sin, but God's promise points to a Savior. The story of redemption starts with hope, even in the middle of rebellion.

Reflection Question: Where in your life have you believed the lie that God is holding something back from you?

Journal Prompt: Write about a time when you tried to hide from God out of shame or guilt. How does His promise in Genesis 3:15 give you hope?

Chapter 3
The First Blood
Genesis 3:21; Hebrews 9:22

Without the shedding of blood there is no forgiveness, Hebrews 9:22

Sin had entered the world.

Adam and Eve listened to the serpent. They ate from the one tree God had forbidden. In doing so, they broke their trust with the Creator. The relationship was shattered. Shame and fear quickly flooded in.

They tried to conceal themselves with fig leaves. They attempted to hide their guilt and solve the problem on their own. But it wasn't enough.

When God confronted them, He not only exposed their sin but also revealed His grace to them. Before sending them out of the garden, He did something unexpected: 'And the Lord God made for Adam and his wife garments of skins and clothed them" (Genesis 3:21).

Where did those skins come from? Scripture does not tell us exactly, but it seems to reason that an animal had to die. Blood had to be shed.

This was the first death, the first blood. It wasn't to punish; it was to cover. The innocent died so the guilty could be clothed.

This moment highlights a key theme throughout the entire Bible: **redemption through substitution**. God didn't overlook sin, but He provided a way for it to be covered, at least temporarily. The animal's blood pointed ahead to a greater sacrifice that was to come.

Every time a lamb was later sacrificed on an altar, every drop of blood in the tabernacle, and every Day of Atonement, all serve as echoes of this moment in the garden. They are also shadows of the cross.

Hebrews 9:22 clearly states, *"Without the shedding of blood there is no* forgiveness." The cost of sin is death. But from the very beginning, God made a way.

The fig leaves weren't enough. Religion, works, effort, and appearance, none of those things can erase sin. Only a substitute can do that. And only God can provide the substitute … Jesus.

Key Scriptures:
- *Genesis 3:21*, garments of skins and clothed them."
- *Hebrews 9:22*, "Without the shedding of blood there is no forgiveness."
- *Leviticus 17:11*, it is the blood that makes atonement by the life."

Lesson: From the beginning, God showed that sin requires a price. But He also showed that He was willing to pay it.

Reflection Question
What affect may it have had on Adam and Eve when they witnessed the death of an innocent animal to cover their shame?

Journal Prompt
Write about a time when you tried to fix a spiritual problem in your life on your own strength. How did that compare to trusting in God's provision?

Chapter 4
The Faithful Remnant Begins
Genesis 4–6

At that time people began to call on the name of the Lord, Genesis 4:26

Sin didn't stop with Adam and Eve. It grew quickly.

Genesis 4 recounts the story of Cain and Abel, their sons. Both brought offerings to God. However, Abel offered the best of his flock, while Cain presented fruit from the ground. God accepted Abel's offering but rejected Cain's. Why? Because Abel's sacrifice was made in faith (Hebrews 11:4). Cain's was not.

Jealousy consumed Cain. Instead of humbling himself, he killed his brother.

It was the first murder, and it stemmed from a heart that refused to listen to God. Sin was already spiraling out of control. Cain was cursed, and his descendants created a godless society. Lamech, one of his descendants, proudly boasted of his violence (Genesis 4:23-24). The world was changing rapidly, and not for the better.

But in the middle of all that darkness, something remarkable happened.

Adam and Eve had another son named Seth. Through his descendants, a new hope appeared. Genesis 4:26 states, *"At that time people began to call on the name of the Lord."* This marks the first sign of a faithful remnant, people who turned back to God and worshiped Him even as the world became more corrupt.

Genesis 5 lists the descendants of Seth, showing a continuous line of people who still walked with God. One name stands out: **Enoch**. Scripture says, *"Enoch walked with God, and he was not, for God took him"* (Genesis 5:24). He never died. God took him home.

However, outside of that remnant, the world continued to slide deeper into evil. Genesis 6:5 says, *"The Lord saw that the wickedness of man was great* in the earth, and that every intention of the thoughts of his heart was only evil continually."

God's heart was broken. Judgment was coming.

Yet even then, God saved a man named **Noah**, a man who *"found favor in the eyes of the Lord"* (Genesis 6:8). The scarlet thread continues, not through the masses, but through the few who still believed.

God has always worked through a faithful remnant. When others walk away, some continue calling on His name. Through them, the story of redemption keeps moving forward.

Key Scriptures:
- *Genesis 4:8*, "Cain rose up against his brother Abel and killed him."
- *Genesis 4:26*, "At that time people began to call on the name of the Lord."
- *Genesis 6:5*, "Every intention … only evil continually."
- *Genesis 6:8*, "But Noah found favor in the eyes of the Lord."

Lesson: Even when sin multiplies, God always preserves a remnant, a few who still trust Him. His plan never dies.

Reflection Question
What does it mean to be part of God's faithful remnant in a world that often ignores Him?

Journal Prompt
Think about an area in your life where you've felt surrounded by darkness or discouragement. How does God's faithfulness to people like Seth, Enoch, and Noah give you hope?

Part Two

The Covenant Path

Chapter 5
Judgment and Grace
Genesis 6–9

But Noah found favor in the eyes of the Lord, Genesis 6:8

The world was unraveling.

People weren't just sinning; they were fully corrupt. Genesis 6:5 says, *"Every inclination of the thoughts of the human heart was only evil all the time."* Violence filled the earth. God grieved that He had made man. But He hadn't given up on redemption.

In the middle of all this evil stood one man: **Noah**.

"Noah was a righteous man, blameless among the people of his time, and he walked faithfully with God" (Genesis 6:9). He wasn't perfect, but he trusted and obeyed the Lord. Because of this, God chose Noah to carry forward His plan of salvation.

God warned him of an approaching judgment, a worldwide flood that would eliminate all life. But He also entrusted Noah with a task: build an ark. It wasn't a small job. It took years. The people around him probably mocked and ignored him. But Noah kept building. And he preached. And he waited.

Finally, the day came. God told Noah to gather his family and pairs of animals into the ark. Then *"the Lord shut him in"* (Genesis 7:16).

Rain poured for forty days and nights. The earth was submerged in water. Every living creature outside the ark was lost. It was a severe, righteous judgment. But inside the ark, there was grace.

When the rain stopped and the waters slowly receded, God made a promise. He placed a rainbow in the sky and *"Never again will I destroy all life with a flood"* (Genesis 9:11).

Noah built an altar and offered a sacrifice. Once again, blood was shed. And once again, God responded with mercy.

The ark is more than just a rescue story; it's a symbol of salvation. The same God who judges sin also offers protection. Just as Noah and his family were rescued through the ark, we are saved through Christ. He is our refuge from the coming judgment.

Key Scriptures:
- *Genesis 6:5,* "Every intention ... only evil continually."
- *Genesis 6:8,* "But Noah found favor in the eyes of the Lord."
- *Genesis 7:16,* "The Lord shut him in."
- *Genesis 8:20,* "Then Noah built an altar to the Lord."
- *Genesis 9:13,* "I have set my bow in the cloud."

Lesson: God must judge sin, but He always provides a way of salvation. The ark points us to Jesus, the only safe place when the floodwaters rise.

Reflection Question
Are you building your life on God's instructions like Noah, or the shifting opinions of the world?

Journal Prompt
Write about what it means for you to take shelter in Christ. What does the ark represent in your own walk with God today?

Chapter 6
Chosen by Grace
Genesis 11:27–2:9, 15, 17

> *I will make you into a great nation ... and all peoples on earth will be blessed through you,* Genesis 12:2–3

After the flood, humanity began to multiply again. But sin remained. People still rejected God, building monuments to their pride, like the Tower of Babel. So God scattered them across the earth (Genesis 11).

Yet God wasn't finished. He was about to initiate a new phase of His plan. Not only would He judge evil, but He would also raise a people through whom redemption would come.

So, He called a man named **Abram**.

Abram wasn't a king or a priest. He wasn't part of a righteous nation. He lived in a pagan land called Ur. But God chose him, not because Abram was great, but because God's grace is great.

God said, *"Go from your country ... to the land that I will show you"* (Genesis 12:1). With that call came a promise:

1. **A Land**, "To your offspring I will give this land" (Genesis 12:7).
2. **A People**, "I will make of you a great nation."
3. **A Blessing**, "In you all the families of the earth shall be blessed."

This wasn't just a personal promise. It was a global mission. The blessing would come through Abram's line, and ultimately through one descendant: **Jesus** (see Galatians 3:16).

Abram obeyed. He left home, ventured into the unknown, and followed God. Later, in Genesis 15, God reaffirmed His promise with a covenant. God asked Abram to prepare a blood sacrifice, and then He alone passed through it, symbolizing that He would uphold the covenant even if Abram failed.

This was grace.

God even changed Abram's name to **Abraham**, meaning *"father of many nations."* And though Abraham had many flaws, he trusted God. Scripture says, *"He believed the Lord, and He counted it to him as righteousness"* (Genesis 15:6). That same kind of faith is what still saves us today.

Key Scriptures:
- *Genesis 12:1–3,* "Go … and I will bless you."
- *Genesis 15:6,* "He believed the Lord."
- *Genesis 17:5,* "Your name shall be Abraham."
- *Galatians 3:8,* "In you shall all the nations be blessed."

Lesson: God's plan of redemption narrowed to one man, one nation, and one future Savior. Salvation has always come by faith, not by works.

Reflection Question
What does Abraham's story teach you about stepping out in faith when God's plan is unclear?

Journal Prompt
Write about a time you sensed God calling you to trust Him, even when the outcome wasn't visible. How did you respond?

Chapter 7
Substitution: Isaac on the Altar
Genesis 22

God himself will provide the lamb for the burnt offering, my son, Genesis 22:8

Abraham had waited for decades for a son. God had promised him descendants "as numerous as the stars," and Isaac was the child through whom that promise would be fulfilled.

Then came the unthinkable.

God said, *"Take your son, your only son Isaac, whom you love … Sacrifice him there as a burnt offering on a mountain I will show you"* (Genesis 22:2–3). No explanation. No details. Just a command. And Abraham obeyed.

He didn't delay. He took Isaac, two servants, and wood for the offering, and set out toward Mount Moriah. The journey lasted three days. On the third day, Abraham saw the mountain and told the servants, *"Stay here … the boy and I will go … and we will come back to you."* Somehow, even then, Abraham believed in God's promise.

As they climbed the mountain, Isaac asked the obvious question: *"Where is the lamb?"* Abraham answered with prophetic faith: *"God will provide for Himself the lamb."*

At the top, Abraham built an altar, arranged the wood, and bound Isaac. He raised the knife.

Then God stopped him.

"Do not lay a hand on the boy…" (Genesis 22:12). And there, caught in a thicket, was a ram. Abraham offered it **in Isaac's place**.

This is one of the clearest examples of **substitution** in the Old Testament. A son was sentenced to death, but a substitute died in his place. This wasn't just about Abraham; it pointed to a future Father and a future Son.

God would one day provide **another lamb**, but this time, there would be no ram in the thicket. Jesus would be the substitute. On the same mountain range (Mount Moriah later became the site of the temple in Jerusalem), God would offer His Son for the sins of the world.

Key Scriptures:
- *Genesis 22:2*, "Take your son … and offer him."
- *Genesis 22:8*, "God will provide the lamb."
- *Genesis 22:13*, "Abraham went and took the ram."
- *John 1:29*, "Behold, the Lamb of God, who takes away the sin of the world!"

Lesson: God provided a substitute for Isaac. He has provided a substitute for you. Jesus took your place.

Reflection Question
What does it mean to you personally that God was willing to sacrifice His own Son for your sin?

Journal Prompt
Write about how the idea of substitution helps you understand both the seriousness of sin and the depth of God's love.

Chapter 8
Providence in Egypt
Genesis 37; 39–50

You intended to harm me, but God intended it for good, Genesis 50:20

The story of Joseph is a clear example of God's providence in all of Scripture. It demonstrates that even when life seems out of control, God is still shaping His plan.

Joseph was Jacob's favorite son. His brothers grew jealous of him. Their jealousy boiled over, and one day they threw him into a pit and sold him to slave traders. Joseph was taken to Egypt, alone, betrayed, and enslaved.

From that point forward, Joseph's life went up and down.

- He rose to oversee his master's household, then was falsely accused and imprisoned.
- He earned favor in prison, then was overlooked by those he assisted.
- Finally, after years of hardship, Joseph was presented to Pharaoh to interpret a troubling dream.

Through God's power, Joseph prophesied an upcoming famine and advised Pharaoh on how to prepare. The Pharaoh promoted him to second-in-command over Egypt.

When the famine struck, it didn't just affect Egypt; it also reached Canaan, where Joseph's family resided. His brothers came to Egypt in search of food, never expecting they would find their long-lost brother on the throne. Joseph had the power to take revenge. Instead, he forgave. He wept. He saved them.

He told them, *"You meant evil against me, but God meant it for good"* (Genesis 50:20). God had used everything, betrayal, slavery, and prison, to bring Joseph to the right place at the right time to preserve His people.

Joseph's story isn't just about enduring pain. It's about recognizing God's hand in it. The scarlet thread runs through him, not because Joseph shed blood, but because he protected the family line through which the Messiah would come.

Key Scriptures:
- *Genesis 37:28,* "They sold him ... for twenty shekels of silver."
- *Genesis 39:2,* "The Lord was with Joseph."
- *Genesis 45:7,* "God sent me before you to preserve life."
- *Genesis 50:20,* "God meant it for good."

Lesson: What others mean for evil; God can use for good. His purpose moves forward, even in the face of pain.

Reflection Question

Can you think of a time in your life when a difficult situation was part of God's greater plan?

Journal Prompt

Write about a painful experience where you later saw signs of God's providence. How did that shape your faith?

Part Three

The Blood That Frees

Chapter 9
The Blood of the Lamb
Exodus 11–12

When I see the blood, I will pass over you, Exodus 12:13

The people of Israel had become slaves in Egypt. For 400 years, they cried out under the weight of oppression. God heard. He remembered His covenant with Abraham. And He raised up a deliverer, **Moses**.

Pharaoh ignored every warning. So, God sent plague after plague, each revealing the emptiness of Egypt's idols. But Pharaoh's heart remained hardened. Then came the final judgment: the death of every firstborn in Egypt.

But this time, God gave Israel specific instructions. Every household was to take a lamb, without blemish, perfect in quality. They were to kill it at twilight and mark their doorposts and lintel with its blood.

That night, the angel of death would pass through Egypt. But wherever the blood was seen, death would pass over.

"When I see the blood, I will pass over you." (Exodus 12:13)

Inside those blood-stained homes, the people were safe. Not because they were better than the Egyptians, but because they were covered by the blood.

This was the **first Passover** and became the defining event of Israel's identity, a story of rescue, judgment, and redemption. Every year, they would remember it. Every year, they would tell their children, *"It is the sacrifice of the Lord's Passover"* (Exodus 12:27).

But the Passover was never just about Egypt; it has always represented something greater.

When John the Baptist saw Jesus walking toward him, he cried out, *"Behold, the Lamb of God, who takes away the sin of the world!"* (John 1:29). Jesus is our Passover Lamb. His blood was shed so that God's judgment would pass over us. His death means our deliverance.

The blood on the doorposts pointed forward to the blood on the cross.

Key Scriptures:
- *Exodus 12:5*, "Your lamb shall be without blemish."
- *Exodus 12:13*, "When I see the blood, I will pass over you."
- *John 1:29*, "Behold, the Lamb of God."
- *1 Corinthians 5:7*, "Christ, our Passover lamb, has been sacrificed."

Lesson: The blood of the lamb didn't just rescue Israel; it prepared the world for Christ. He is the Lamb whose blood still saves.

Reflection Question
How does the Passover help you understand the seriousness of sin and the cost of salvation?

Journal Prompt
Write about what it means that Jesus, the perfect Lamb, died in your place. How does that truth shape how you approach God?

Chapter 10
The Tabernacle and Sacrifice
Exodus 25–40; Leviticus 1, 16–17

It is the blood that makes atonement for one's life, Leviticus 17:11

After Israel was freed from Egypt, God led them to Mount Sinai. There, He gave them not only His law but also a place to meet Him.

That place was the **tabernacle**, a sacred tent in the wilderness where God's presence dwelled among His people. Every detail carried meaning. Every object pointed to something greater. And at the center of it all was this truth: **you cannot approach a holy God without a sacrifice**.

God instructed Israel to bring animals, bulls, goats, lambs, as offerings. These animals had to be **without blemish**, pure, and healthy. Their blood was poured out at the altar. Why? Because sin causes death, and blood symbolizes the price being paid.

As Leviticus says, *"It is the blood that makes atonement by the life"* (Leviticus 17:11).

Once a year on **the Day of Atonement**, the high priest entered the Most Holy Place. He carried blood and sprinkled it on the mercy seat of the Ark of the Covenant. This wasn't symbolic; it was sacred. Without it, there was no covering for the people's sins.

This system may seem foreign to us now, but it was God's way of teaching a vital lesson: **you can't take sin lightly**, and **you can't remove guilt on your own**. Only by substitution, only through blood, could forgiveness be achieved.

But the tabernacle was only temporary. The blood needed to be offered repeatedly. Hebrews 10:4 states, *"It is impossible for the blood of bulls and goats to take away sins."* These sacrifices weren't the ultimate solution. They were a shadow, a glimpse of the real sacrifice to come.

Jesus is both our high priest and our sacrifice. When He died, the curtain of the temple was torn in two. The system of repeated offerings was fulfilled. His blood was sufficient, once and for all.

Key Scriptures:
- *Exodus 25:8,* "Let them make Me a sanctuary, that I may dwell among them."
- *Leviticus 17:11,* "The life of the flesh is in the blood."
- *Hebrews 9:12,* "He entered once for all … by means of His own blood."
- *Hebrews 10:10,* "We have been sanctified … through the offering of the body of Jesus Christ once for all."

Lesson: God made a way to dwell with His people, but it required blood. Jesus is the perfect sacrifice who fulfilled what the tabernacle only foreshadowed.

Reflection Question
Why do you think God used such a detailed and costly system to deal with sin in the Old Testament?

Journal Prompt
Write about how understanding the sacrificial system deepens your appreciation for what Jesus did on the cross.

Chapter 11
The Wilderness Test
Numbers 13–14; Deuteronomy 1; Psalm 106

How long will these people treat me with contempt? How long will they refuse to believe in me, in spite of all the signs I have performed among them?
Number 14:11

Israel had seen the power of God firsthand.

They watched Him part the Red Sea. They followed a pillar of fire by night. They received bread from heaven and water from rocks. They heard His voice at Mount Sinai. They carried the ark of His presence and saw His cloud cover the tabernacle.

But when it was time to enter the Promised Land, they froze.

God told Moses to send twelve spies to scout the land. It was exactly as God had promised: rich, fertile, abundant. But ten of the twelve spies came back terrified. *"We can't take it,"* they said. *"The people are giants. The cities are too strong."*

Only Joshua and Caleb believed. *"If the Lord delights in us,"* they said, *"He will give it to us."*

But the people refused to trust. They cried out in fear, wished to return to Egypt, and even talked about choosing a new leader.

God had every reason to destroy them, but Moses begged for mercy. God relented, yet it came with consequences.

The generation that refused to believe would not enter the land. For forty years, they wandered in the wilderness until that unbelieving generation died out. Their children would inherit what they had rejected.

This was more than a delay. It was a judgment on disbelief.

Throughout their wilderness journey, the people complained, rebelled, tested God, and worshiped idols. Yet, God continued to provide. He gave food, water, leadership, and forgiveness. He never abandoned them, even when they failed Him.

The wilderness teaches us that redemption isn't the conclusion, **faithfulness is**. Salvation results in testing, and testing shows whether we really trust the One who saves us.

Key Scriptures:
- *Numbers 13:30*, "Let us go up at once ... for we are well able to overcome it."
- *Numbers 14:11*, "How long will they not believe in Me?"
- *Numbers 14:20*, "I have pardoned, according to your word."
- *Psalm 106:13*, "They soon forgot His works."

Lesson: Redemption leads to testing. Faith grows or shrinks in the wilderness. God is faithful even when we are not.

Reflection Question
Why do you think fear so often overpowers faith, even after we've seen God work?

Journal Prompt
Think about a time when you felt spiritually stuck in the wilderness. What did you learn about God's mercy and your own faith?

Chapter 12
Rahab and the Scarlet Cord
Joshua 2; 6:22–25

[Tie] this scarlet cord in the window ... and you (and your family will live),
Joshua 2:18

The people of Israel stood on the border of the Promised Land again, forty years after their initial failure to believe. This time, they were ready. Joshua had taken charge. The new generation had been prepared.

But the land was still full of danger. The city of **Jericho** stood tall and strong, its walls thick, its army alert.

Joshua sent two spies into the city to gather information. They took shelter in an unexpected place: the house of a prostitute named **Rahab**.

Rahab had heard of Israel's God. She knew what He had done to Egypt. She knew the Red Sea had parted, and she believed that He would give the land to His people.

In faith, she hid the spies from the king's men and safely sent them away. But before they left, she asked for one thing: salvation. *"Please ... spare my family,"* she said (Joshua 2:12–13).

The spies agreed. If she tied a **scarlet cord** in her window and kept her family inside, they would be spared when the city fell.

And when the day arrived, when the walls of Jericho fell and Israel stormed through, Rahab's house remained standing. The scarlet cord still hung in the window, and everyone inside was saved.

The blood wasn't literal this time, but the symbol was unmistakable. A **scarlet sign** marked the house of safety. Rahab believed, and her faith led to action. Just like in Egypt during the Passover, judgment passed over the home that was covered.

Rahab evolved from a survivor to a member of Israel. And not just that, she became part of the line of Christ (Matthew 1:5).

From prostitute to ancestor of the Messiah, because she trusted the God of Israel and took refuge in His mercy.

Key Scriptures:
- *Joshua 2:11,* "The Lord your God, He is God in the heavens above and on the earth beneath."
- *Joshua 2:18,* "Tie this scarlet cord in the window."
- *Joshua 6:25,* "Rahab ... lived in Israel to this day."
- *Hebrews 11:31,* "By faith Rahab ... did not perish."
- *Matthew 1:5,* "Salmon fathered Boaz by Rahab."

Lesson: No one is too far from God. Rahab's scarlet cord shows that salvation is by faith, and God delights in rescuing the unlikely.

Reflection Question
What does Rahab's story teach you about how God sees people others often overlook?

Journal Prompt
Think about the "scarlet cord" moments in your life, times when you trusted God even when everything around you seemed against you. What did He do through your faith?

Chapter 13
Kings, Sin, and Prophets
1 Samuel–2 Kings; 2 Chronicles 36; Isaiah 1

They have forsaken the Lord; they have spurned the Holy One of Israel and turned their backs on him, Isaiah 1:4

Israel had entered the land. They had seen God bring down walls, conquer enemies, and divide territory. But faith often fades quickly when comfort increases.

After Joshua's death, a pattern emerged: rebellion, judgment, repentance, deliverance, and then rebellion again. This cycle repeated through the time of the **judges**, when *"everyone did what was right in his own eyes"* (Judges 21:25).

Eventually, the people wanted a king. Not God as king, but a human king, *"like all the other nations"* (1 Samuel 8:5). God gave them Saul, then David, then Solomon.

David was a man after God's own heart. He worshiped, wrote psalms, and longed to build a house for God. But even David sinned greatly. Solomon, his son, started with wisdom and peace, but his many wives led him into idolatry.

After Solomon's death, the kingdom was **divided**, Israel in the north and Judah in the south. Both nations moved away from God. Idolatry became commonplace. Injustice spread throughout. Worship lost its meaning. They still made sacrifices, but their hearts were distant from God.

God didn't stay silent. He sent **prophets**, including Isaiah, Jeremiah, Hosea, and Micah, among many others. These messengers called the people to repent, warned of judgment, and reminded them of the covenant. They also spoke of a coming Savior.

But the people refused to listen. Repeatedly, the prophets cried out, *"Return to the Lord!"* Repeatedly, the people hardened their hearts.

Eventually, judgment arrived. The northern kingdom fell to Assyria first, and later, Babylon conquered the southern kingdom. Jerusalem was burned, the temple was destroyed, and the people were exiled, just as God had warned.

But even then, the scarlet thread remained uncut. In exile, the prophets continued to speak of **hope**. Of a new covenant. Of a faithful servant. Of a day when God would restore His people, not just outwardly, but from the heart.

Key Scriptures:
- *1 Samuel 8:7*, "They have rejected Me from being king over them."
- *1 Kings 11:4*, "His heart was not wholly true to the Lord."
- *Isaiah 1:18*, "Though your sins are like scarlet, they shall be white as snow."
- *2 Chronicles 36:16*, "They kept mocking the messengers of God."

Lesson: God is patient, but sin has consequences. Still, He always leaves a thread of hope, even in judgment.

Reflection Question
Why do people often drift from God during times of prosperity or comfort?

Journal Prompt
Write about a time you resisted God's correction. What did He use to call you back, and what did you learn through it?

Chapter 14
Foreshadowing the Cross
Isaiah 52–53; Zechariah 12–13

He was pierced for our transgressions, he was crushed for our iniquities,
Isaiah 53:5

As Israel's sins grew, so did the prophets' cries, not only of warning but also of **hope**.

As judgment approached, someone greater was also on the way. A **Servant**, sent by God. One who would not come with armies or chariots, but with sorrow, rejection, and pain. One who would bear the guilt of others.

In **Isaiah 52–53**, we meet this Servant.

He would be *"despised and rejected by men"*, *"a man of sorrows"*, familiar with grief. He wouldn't be outwardly impressive. People would turn away from Him. Yet, *"He has borne our griefs and carried our sorrows."*

Isaiah doesn't say the Servant would suffer for His own sin, but for ours.

"He was pierced for our transgressions, crushed for our iniquities… and the Lord has laid on Him the iniquity of us all." (Isaiah 53:5-6)

It is one of the clearest pictures of the cross, written over **700 years before Jesus was born**.

The Servant remained silent before His accusers. He would be cut off from the land of the living. He would be given a grave with the wicked yet be buried with the rich. Every detail aligns with Jesus' death and burial.

And yet, Isaiah also says: *"He shall see His offspring; He shall prolong His days."* Death would not be the end.

Zechariah adds to this vision by describing a day when God's people will *"look on Me, on Him whom they have pierced"* (Zechariah 12:10). Mourning will happen, but there will also be a **fountain for cleansing**, a fountain opened *"to cleanse them from sin and uncleanness"* (Zechariah 13:1).

The prophets saw the cross from afar. They didn't know His name. They didn't know the shape of the wood. But they knew **a sacrifice** was coming. One final and perfect. The thread was pulling tighter.

Key Scriptures:
- Isaiah 52:13—53:12, "He poured out His soul to death ... yet He bore the sin of many."
- Zechariah 12:10, "They will look on Me, the one they have pierced."
- Zechariah 13:1, "On that day a fountain will be opened ... to cleanse."
- 1 Peter 2:24, "He Himself bore our sins in His body on the tree."

Lesson: The cross wasn't a surprise. It was God's plan from the beginning, foretold in detail, fulfilled in Christ.

Reflection Question

How does knowing that Jesus' suffering was prophesied hundreds of years earlier deepen your understanding of the cross?

Journal Prompt

Write a response to Isaiah 53 in your own words. What part of that prophecy stands out most to you, and why?

Part Four

The Coming of the Redeemer

Chapter 15
The Lamb Has Come
John 1; Luke 2; Matthew 1–2

Look, the Lamb of God, who takes away the sin of the world, John 1:29

For centuries, Israel had waited.

They remembered the promise to Abraham: "In you all the families of the earth shall be blessed."

They recalled the Servant in Isaiah, the pierced One in Zechariah, the King from David's line, and the Redeemer to come.

Then, in a quiet town and to an ordinary girl, the promise took on flesh.

Jesus was born, not in a palace, but in a stable. Not welcomed by kings, but by shepherds. Not with fanfare, but with humility.

He was fully human, born of Mary. Yet fully divine, conceived by the Holy Spirit. *"They shall call His name Immanuel, which means, 'God with us.'"* (Matthew 1:23)

Jesus didn't come just to teach, heal, or lead a movement. He came to **fulfill** everything the scarlet thread pointed to. From the lamb in Eden, to the blood in Egypt, to the words of the prophets, **He was the Lamb all along**.

John the Baptist understood. When he saw Jesus approaching, he didn't say, "Behold, the Teacher." He didn't say, "Behold, the King." He said,

"Behold, the Lamb of God, who takes away the sin of the world!" (John 1:29)

Jesus was born to die. Even as a baby, He was marked by the cross. Simeon told Mary that a sword would pierce her soul. Herod tried to kill Him, and wise men brought Him gifts, including **myrrh** for burial.

The Lamb had come. Not to be admired, but to be offered.

Key Scriptures:
- *Luke 2:11*, "For unto you is born ... a Savior, who is Christ the Lord."
- *John 1:14*, "The Word became flesh and dwelt among us."
- *John 1:29*, "Behold, the Lamb of God."
- *Matthew 2:11*, "They offered Him gifts ... gold, frankincense, and myrrh."

Lesson: Jesus is the fulfillment of every promise, prophecy, and picture in Scripture. He is the Lamb, given to take away our sins.

Reflection Question

Why do you think God chose to send Jesus in such a quiet and humble way?

Journal Prompt

Imagine yourself in the crowd when John called Jesus the Lamb of God. What would that have meant to you? What does it mean to you now?

Chapter 16
The Lamb Takes Our Place
John 19; Matthew 26–27; Isaiah 53; Hebrews 9

He himself bore our sins in his body on the cross so that we might die to sins and live for righteousness, 1 Peter 2:24

The moment had come.

Jesus, the Lamb, promised, foreshadowed, prophesied, and was about to be slain. Not because of failure, but because of faithfulness. Not because of weakness, but because of love.

In the garden of Gethsemane, He prayed, *My Father, if it is possible, may this cup be taken from me. Yet not as I will, but as you will,* Matthew 26:39.

He was betrayed, arrested, beaten, mocked, and falsely accused. The very people He came to save shouted, *"Crucify Him!"* Soldiers drove nails through His hands and feet. They lifted Him up on a cross between two criminals.

This wasn't an accident. It wasn't a tragedy. It was **the plan**.

Isaiah had seen it long before:

But he was pierced for our transgressions, he was crushed for our iniquities; the punishment that brought us peace was on him, and by his wounds we are healed. We all, like sheep, have gone astray, each of us has turned to our own way; and the Lord has laid on him the iniquity of us all, Isaiah 53:5–6.

Jesus didn't just die; **He died in our place**.
    The righteous for the unrighteous.
    The holy for the unholy.
    The innocent for the guilty.

Hebrews tells us that without the shedding of blood, there is no forgiveness (Hebrews 9:22). However, unlike the blood of animals, which had to be offered repeatedly, **Jesus' blood was final**.

And by that will, we have been made holy through the sacrifice of the body of Jesus Christ once for all, Hebrews 10:10.

At the very moment He died, the veil in the temple was torn in two, from top to bottom. The barrier between God and man was removed. The price was paid. The way was open.

Jesus' final words: *"It is finished."* (John 19:30). Not "I am finished," but **"It is."** The debt of sin. The curse of the law. The punishment we deserved. Finished.

Key Scriptures:
- *Matthew 26:39*, "Not My will, but Yours be done."
- *Isaiah 53:5-6*, "The Lord has laid on Him the iniquity of us all."
- *John 19:30*, "It is finished."
- *Hebrews 10:10*, "Once for all."

Lesson: Jesus didn't just die; He died for you. The cross wasn't a symbol of defeat. It was the greatest act of love and the final payment for sin.

Reflection Question
How do you personally respond to the reality that Jesus took your place on the cross?

Journal Prompt
Write a prayer of thanksgiving to Jesus for what He endured for you. What does "It is finished" mean in your life right now?

Chapter 17
Risen and Reigning
Luke 24; John 20; 1 Corinthians 15; Revelation 1

Why do you look for the living among the dead? He is not here; he has risen! Remember how he told you, while he was still with you in Galilee, Luke 24:5–6

Jesus was crucified. Buried. Wrapped in linen and laid in a sealed tomb.

The world grew silent. The disciples scattered. Hope seemed lost.

But then came the third day.

At sunrise, women went to the tomb with spices, only to find the stone rolled away. Two angels greeted them with the greatest words ever spoken:

"He is not here, he has risen." (Luke 24:6)

Jesus appeared, alive. First to Mary, then to His disciples, and later to over 500 people (1 Corinthians 15:6). He spoke, ate, walked, and taught. The Lamb who was slain had become **the risen King**.

The resurrection wasn't just symbolic. It was physical, bodily, verified, and it changed everything.

It proved that Jesus was who He claimed to be, the Son of God. It confirmed that the cross worked, the payment for sin was accepted. It broke the power of death, offering eternal life to all who believe. Paul declared,

> *And if Christ has not been raised, your faith is futile; you are still in your sins. But Christ has indeed been raised from the dead, the firstfruits of those who have fallen asleep,* 1 Corinthians 15:17, 20.

The resurrection changed weeping into joy, fear into courage, and defeat into purpose. The disciples who once hid behind locked doors now preached openly in the streets. Why? Because they had seen the risen Lord.

In Revelation 1, John sees Jesus in glory and falls at His feet. But Jesus says,

> *Do not be afraid. I am the First and the Last. I am the Living One; I was dead, and now look, I am alive forever and ever! And I hold the keys of death and Hades,* Revelation 1:17–18.

The scarlet thread didn't end at the cross. It shines in resurrection power. The Lamb lives, and He reigns.

Key Scriptures:
- *Luke 24:6,* "He is not here, but has risen."
- *John 20:27–28,* "My Lord and my God!"
- *1 Corinthians 15:20,* "Christ has been raised from the dead."
- *Revelation 1:18,* "I am alive forevermore."

Lesson: The cross paid for sin. The resurrection proved the payment was accepted. Jesus is alive, and because He lives, we have hope that cannot die.

Reflection Question
What does Jesus' resurrection mean for how you face death, suffering, or uncertainty?

Journal Prompt
Write about a part of your life where you need to remember that Jesus is alive and reigning. How does His resurrection relate to that situation?

Chapter 18
The Gospel Goes Out
Acts 1–2; 9; Ephesians 2; Revelation 5

> *For you know that it was not with perishable things such as silver or gold that you were redeemed from the empty way of life handed down to you from your ancestors, but with the precious blood of Christ, a lamb without blemish or defect,*
> 1 Peter 1:18–19

After His resurrection, Jesus gathered His disciples and gave them a mission: "You will be My witnesses ... to the end of the earth." (Acts 1:8)

Then He ascended. But He didn't leave them alone.

Ten days later, on the day of Pentecost, the Holy Spirit arrived with power. Tongues of fire rested on the apostles. They spoke in many languages. A crowd gathered. And Peter stood up and preached.

This same Peter who once denied Jesus now boldly proclaimed Him:

> *God has made Him both Lord and Christ, this Jesus whom you crucified.* (Acts 2:36)

The people were cut to the heart. *"What shall we do?"* they asked.

Peter answered, *"Repent and be baptized ... for the forgiveness of your sins."* That day, 3,000 people believed and were added to the church. The gospel had begun to spread.

But it wasn't just Jews. God soon called Saul, a persecutor of Christians, and transformed him into **Paul**, the apostle to the Gentiles. Paul traveled across the Roman Empire, writing letters, planting churches, and sharing one central message:

"We have redemption through His blood, the forgiveness of sins." (Ephesians 1:7)

From Jerusalem to Antioch, Corinth to Rome, the scarlet thread connected diverse cultures and continents. The church grew not through military force or politics, but through the message of the cross and the power of the Spirit.

In Revelation 5, John sees a vision of heaven. Multitudes fall before the throne, singing:

> *Worthy are You… for You were slain, and by Your blood You ransomed people for God from every tribe and language and people and nation.* (Revelation 5:9)

The story of redemption had gone global.

Key Scriptures:
- *Acts 1:8*, "You will be My witnesses."
- *Acts 2:38*, "Repent and be baptized."
- *Ephesians 1:7*, "In Him we have redemption through His blood."
- *Revelation 5:9*, "You ransomed people … by Your blood."

Lesson: The gospel is for all people. Jesus's blood didn't just change history, it changed hearts around the world, one life at a time.

Reflection Question

Why do you think God chose to spread the message of the cross through people like Peter, Paul, and now, through us?

Journal Prompt

Who in your life needs to hear the gospel? Ask God to give you an open door and a bold heart to share the hope of Christ's blood.

Chapter 19
Atonement Explained
Romans 3–5; 2 Corinthians 5; Hebrews 9–10

But God demonstrates his own love for us in this: While we were still sinners, Christ died for us, Romans 5:8

The cross was not only a moment of suffering, but it was also the center of God's eternal plan.

Jesus didn't just die as a martyr; He died as a substitute. The apostles didn't just record the events; they explained what they meant.

Paul teaches that *"all have sinned and fall short of the glory of God"* (Romans 3:23). Yet, God presented Jesus *"as a propitiation by His blood"* (Romans 3:25). The word **propitiation** means Jesus took the wrath we deserved. He stood in our place, so we could stand in grace.

> *He made Him who knew no sin to be sin on our behalf, so that we might become the righteousness of God.* (2 Corinthians 5:21)

This is the core of the gospel: **Jesus took our place.** His blood satisfied justice and paved the way for reconciliation.

But how do we enter this grace?

Scripture clearly states **we must respond to the gospel.** We are saved **by grace** (Ephesians 2:8), but we access that grace **through obedient faith,** not by works we invent, but by the response God commands.

When the people at Pentecost believed the gospel, they cried out, *"What shall we do?"* Peter didn't say, "Just believe." He said,

> *Repent and be baptized every one of you in the name of Jesus Christ for the forgiveness of your sins.* (Acts 2:38)

Baptism is not a human act; it is a surrender of faith. Paul said that in baptism we are united with Christ in His death and raised to walk in newness of life (Romans 6:3–4). It is the moment we die to sin and are clothed with Christ (Galatians 3:27).

Jesus' blood washes away sin, but **baptism is how that washing is received** (Acts 22:16).

This isn't salvation through ritual; it's salvation by grace, received through **faith that obeys**. A faith that declares, "Not my will, but Yours be done."

The scarlet thread brings us here: Jesus took your place and now invites you to die with Him, be buried with Him, and rise with Him.

Key Scriptures:
- *Romans 3:23–25*, "Justified by His grace … through faith … by His blood."
- *Acts 2:38*, "Repent and be baptized … for the forgiveness of your sins."
- *Romans 6:3–4*, "Baptized into His death … raised to walk in newness of life."
- *Acts 22:16*, "Be baptized and wash away your sins, calling on His name."

Lesson: Salvation is a gift, paid for by Christ's blood and received through obedient faith. Baptism is where faith meets grace, and the sinner meets the Savior.

Reflection Question
How does baptism express both surrender and trust in the power of Jesus' death and resurrection?

Journal Prompt
If you've been baptized into Christ, write about what that day meant to you. If you haven't, what's holding you back?

Chapter 20
The Final Victory
Revelation 5; 7; 21–22

They have washed their robes and made them white in the blood of the Lamb,
Revelation 7:14

The story that began in a garden ends in a city.

In Genesis, sin entered the world, and humanity was driven away from God's presence. In Revelation, sin is overcome, and the redeemed are welcomed into **God's eternal dwelling**.

John's vision in Revelation shows us the final scene of the scarlet thread:

- A throne.
- A Lamb standing as though slain.
- Multitudes from every nation singing a new song: *"Worthy is the Lamb who was slain."* (Revelation 5:12)

They are no longer suffering. No longer afraid. No longer stained by sin.

These are they who have come out of the great tribulation; they have washed their robes and made them white in the blood of the Lamb. (Revelation 7:14)

White, because of blood. Pure, because of sacrifice. Victorious, because of Jesus.

The Bible ends with a promise:

> *He will wipe every tear from their eyes. There will be no more death' or mourning or crying or pain, for the old order of things has passed away.* (Revelation 21:4).

And the voice from the throne declares:

> "I am making everything new!" Then he said, "Write this down, for these words are trustworthy and true." (Revelation 21:5).

There is no temple in this city because God resides there. No sun or moon because the Lamb is its light. No curse because sin has been removed.

This is the final victory. The redeemed, blood-washed people of God, **forever with Him**.

The thread has run from Eden to Egypt, from a ram on the mountain to a cross on a hill. And now, it shines in glory.

Key Scriptures:
- *Revelation 5:9*, "By Your blood You ransomed people for God."
- *Revelation 7:14*, "Washed their robes ... in the blood of the Lamb."
- *Revelation 21:4*, "He will wipe away every tear."
- *Revelation 22:14*, "Blessed are those who wash their robes."

Lesson: The Lamb who was slain is now the King who reigns. All who trust Him, follow Him, and are washed in His blood will live with Him forever.

Reflection Question
How does the promise of eternity with God shape the way you live today?

Journal Prompt
Write a personal response to the Lamb who was slain, and now reigns. What are you most looking forward to in His presence?

Your Place in the Story

From the first page of Scripture to the last, God has been telling one story.

It's not a story of perfect people earning their way back to Him. It's the story of a perfect God pursuing broken people with relentless grace.

The scarlet thread we've followed is not just a theme; it is **the backbone of the Bible**. It ties together creation and covenant, law and love, prophets and promises, cross and crown. It reveals the heart of God: **to redeem**.

Every lamb, every altar, every drop of blood was pointing forward.

> To Jesus.
> To the Lamb of God.
> To the cross where justice and mercy met.
> To the empty tomb where death was defeated.
> To the church, where that message goes out to all.
> And to heaven, where the redeemed will sing forever: *"Worthy is the Lamb who was slain."*

This story is not just something to admire. It demands a response.

- Will you trust the blood of the Lamb?
- Will you be washed, made new, and walk in the light of His grace?
- Will you carry this thread into your own life, letting it shape your faith, your hope, your future?

The invitation still stands. The blood still speaks. The Lamb still reigns.

And the story is not over.

> *To him who loves us and has freed us from our sins by his blood, and has made us to be a kingdom and priests to serve his God and Father, to him be glory and power for ever and ever! Amen,* Revelation 1:5–6.

Author Biographies

MATTHEW ALLEN lives in Waynesville, Ohio, and has served as the pulpit minister for Cornerstone Church of Christ in Centerville (Dayton), Ohio, since 2010 and has been preaching since 1995. Besides Matthew's local and domestic ministerial work, he has been blessed to do mission work in Ukraine, Canada, Belize, and Colombia. He has also directed several men's retreats nationwide. Matthew owns Spiritbuilding Publishers, leads *Your Pathway Home*—a live, interactive, worldwide webcast by Cornerstone Church of Christ—and publishes the online blog *From Fear to Faith*.

RUSS ROBINS is a lifelong Ohioan, raised on a farm near West Jefferson and now living in Sugar Creek Township. After working in food service and spending over 20 years in the water treatment industry, Russ became the owner of High-Tech Floor Coatings in Dayton. He and his wife, Yvonna, have been married since 1978 and are blessed with five grown children: Seth, Brittney, Brandon, Tori, and Taylor. Russ has faithfully served the Cornerstone church family since 2008, first as a deacon and since 2010 as an elder. His greatest desire is to help others reach heaven and one day rejoice together around God's throne, finally home.

KYLE FLETCHER, a native of eastern Kentucky, is currently serving as an Active-Duty Marine stationed at Wright-Patterson Air Force Base in Dayton, Ohio. He began his ministry journey three years ago and now travels across Kentucky, Ohio, West Virginia, and North Carolina to preach and teach the Gospel. In 2024, he joined the Cornerstone Church of Christ family. Kyle and his wife, Angela, have two daughters, Eliza and Nora, and reside in Beavercreek, Ohio.

www.ingramcontent.com/pod-product-compliance
Lightning Source LLC
LaVergne TN
LVHW010319070426
835510LV00031B/3454